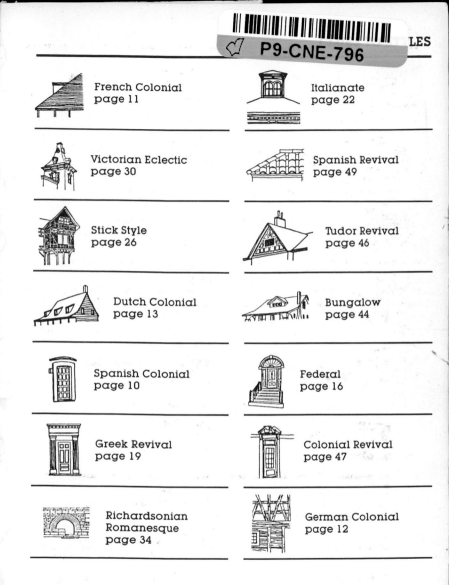

CLUES
to
American
Architecture

63 ill
Marilyn W. Klein 18 cm
David P. Fogle
Illustrated by Wolcott B. Etienne

STARRHILL PRESS
Washington DC

Published by Starrhill Press
P.O. Box 32342
Washington, DC 20007

Library of Congress Cataloging in Publication Data

Klein, Marilyn W.
Clues to American Architecture

1. Architecture—United States—Details.   I. Fogle,
David P.   II. Title.
NA705.K56 1985   720′.973   85-50840
ISBN 0-913515-10-8 (pbk.)

Published simultaneously in Canada by Fitzhenry & Whiteside, Toronto

The drawings for this book are based on photographs
and drawings from the collection of the Historic American Buildings
Survey, U.S. Department of the Interior; on slides from the
collection of the University of Maryland, School of
Architecture; on slides and photographs from the authors'
personal collections; and on photographs taken
by Deborah Klein and Stephen Klein.

The authors would like to acknowledge the generous
assistance of Elizabeth Alley, slide curator at the School
of Architecture, University of Maryland.

Printed in the United States of America

First edition

1 3 5 7 6 4 2

TABLE OF CONTENTS

132072

6 FORWARD

This addition to the writings on American architecture brings the subject to the user in a readily comprehensible format. Its authors' intent has been to make it a factual but concise and popular guide to American building over three centuries. Although it presents the "high style" characteristics of various architectural forms, an understanding of such stylistic touchstones is mandatory to recognizing more vernacular interpretations. The latter, as often as not, are the design forms that the architectural observer is more likely to meet on the streetscapes of America.

Of primary usefulness is the clear presentation of architectural detail which the drawings in this small volume offer. Drawings such as these communicate beyond a shadow of a doubt the precise qualities of any given style, details of which are often lost in photographs. These, combined with the easy-to-comprehend text, offer the architectural amateur and professional alike a handy reference tool, in small format, readily available for on-the-spot reference.

William S. Murtagh

Alexandria, Virginia
May, 1985

   Interest in the natural and the built environment has intensified in America in the last twenty years. Formerly neglectful and destructive of the environment, we are increasingly mindful and protective of it today.

   At the root of an appreciation of the built environment and of the simple enjoyment of looking at buildings is a basic knowledge of architectural history and styles. This small book is intended as an easy-to-use introduction to the most prevalent types of American architecture from colonial times to the present. Its concise format with brief informative descriptions and line drawings should make it easy for anyone to become an architectural detective. The "clues" to each style are the architectural details—such as windows, doors, porches, roof lines—shown in the 'look fors' at the bottom of each page, in the main examples, and on the inside covers. These clues will encourage the reader to look closely at buildings, to appreciate their special qualities and sources of inspiration, and to savor our varied and alive architectural heritage.

   In exploring your neighborhood or wandering down city streets with this book in your pocket, you will find buildings that do not fit neatly into the categories we have defined, as their builders or architects mixed features of several styles. In some cases different styles have some similar characteristics, while in others, buildings are highly individual. Thus, not all would agree about how to characterize a particular building. This will provide a special challenge to the reader to determine which style most appropriately describes a particular building.

   At the end of the book are blank pages for your special finds and for your own insights. In addition to the architectural types we have discussed, you may find examples of current trends, such as older buildings or facades with modern additions, the new "Victorian" houses being built today, and contemporary high-rise atrium designs that attempt to provide public spaces in commercial buildings. We now invite you to use this book to discover, for yourself, clues to American architecture.

Marilyn W. Klein
David P. Fogle

The most numerous and influential colonists were the English merchants and farmers who settled the Massachusetts Bay Colony. The small towns and rural villages they left behind in southeastern England had developed gradually, but the New England towns they established were America's first planned communities — a creation of order cleared within the woods. Houses were clustered around a green, or "common", and a meeting house that served as the religious and community center for the village. Using the plentiful wood from the forests, the Puritan carpenters built their boxlike houses in the familiar way they had known in England: two rooms wide and one or two rooms deep, with two stories. A lean-to added to the back of the house, with the roof lowered to cover it, formed a saltbox shape. Houses originally built with a lean-to had a continuous roof plane. Some houses had a second-story overhang, or "jetty", to create more space upstairs. Heavy oak-timber frames were covered with unpainted clapboards or shingles for protection from winter winds. Steeply pitched shingled roofs shed the heavy snows, and a massive central chimney warmed the house. Heavy doors and small high leaded casement windows guarded against Indian attack. Ornament was considered an expression of vanity, and the only decorations were carved pendants, or "pendills", hanging from corners.

More than seventy examples of this early Colonial style remain in New England today, mostly in Massachusetts and Connecticut. This simple, sculptural form, with its weathered gray shingles, has been used up to the present time in seaside settings. (MWK)

LOOK FOR:

tall chimney and
saltbox shape
(above, right)

sometimes
paneled front
door (above, right)

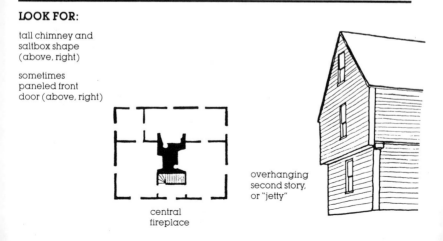

central
fireplace

overhanging
second story,
or "jetty"

Ogden House, Fairfield, Connecticut, c. 1700

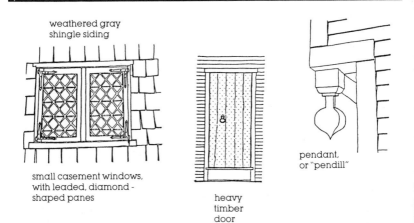

weathered gray
shingle siding

small casement windows,
with leaded, diamond -
shaped panes

heavy
timber
door

pendant,
or "pendill"

In 1548, Phillip II of Spain established the Law of the Indies detailing the layout and physical characteristics of Spanish settlements in the New World. Remnants of the formula are still to be seen in Spanish settlements in North America from St. Augustine, Florida, to Los Angeles, California. Notable examples of this architecture remain in such places as San Antonio, Santa Fe and the California coast, in churches and domestic buildings. The mission complexes in California and the Southwest derive from Spanish Baroque churches of the 16th century, extending north from the colonial centers of New Spain in Mexico. The style and methods of construction continued relatively unchanged until the 19th century. Influenced also by American Indian architecture, the structures were made of adobe or mud bricks with expanses of blank wall punctured by small windows with solid wood shutters. Roofs are supported by wooden beams, sometimes painted and held by decorative brackets, or "zapatas". St. Augustine, Florida, claims the oldest house in the United States, a Spanish Colonial, dating from the late 16th century. (DPF)

Casa Amesti, Monterey, California, c. 1834
Builder: José Amesti

LOOK FOR:

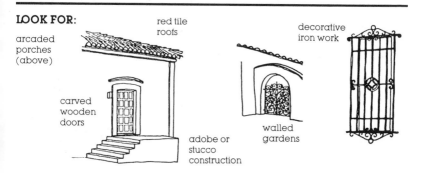

arcaded porches (above)

red tile roofs

carved wooden doors

adobe or stucco construction

walled gardens

decorative iron work

During the 18th century, French Colonial architecture followed the establishment of towns by French settlers in the St. Lawrence and Mississippi River valleys and around the Great Lakes. After the Louisiana Purchase of 1803, the style declined except in the Mississippi Delta. Most surviving examples are located in Louisiana and Mississippi, with a concentration in New Orleans' French Quarter (Vieux Carre). A characteristic example is a pavilion structure with a high pitched roof and paired French doors with transoms flanked by vertical board shutters on strap hinges. These doors are casemented windows which open to allow access to a terrace or balcony. Construction was generally of half-timbered walls, infilled with rubble, clay or bricks, and stuccoed on the surface. High roofs extended beyond buildings to cover long porches or galleries, often two-storied. Used for a number of plantation houses in the Mississippi River Delta, this style is also seen in small urban houses in Mississippi Valley towns. (DPF)

Homeplace Plantation, Hahnville, Louisiana, 1810

LOOK FOR:

narrow
dormer
windows
(above)

double French
doors or windows
with shutters

steep
roofs

pavilion structure

long
gallery

In about 1680, the first German colonists arrived in William Penn's colony seeking religious freedom. Information about tolerance there had been disseminated in Europe, in pamphlets printed in English, French, Dutch, and German. The German immigrants created orderly settlements, building solid rectangular houses in the German medieval tradition—often with central chimneys, steep shingled roofs, and thick stone walls, using fieldstone or limestone from nearby quarries. Half-timbered and wood construction were also used, but less frequently. A pent roof to shelter the first floor is common. An example with wood construction and shed dormers (Ephrata Cloister, Ephrata, Pennsylvania, 1735-49) is shown below. German Colonial buildings can be found principally in Pennsylvania, and in western Maryland. German Colonial buildings took on Georgian features as the influence of English styles spread through the colonies. (MWK)

John Johnson House, Germantown, Philadelphia, Pennsylvania, 1768

LOOK FOR:

fieldstone exterior, two stories (above)

pent roof over the first floor (above)

windows with many panes (above)

half-timbering

steeply pitched shingled roof with shed dormers

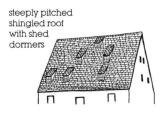

In the early years of the 17th century, Huguenot settlers came through Holland from France to the New World in search of religious tolerance. They settled as traders around the Hudson and Delaware Rivers, building their Dutchlike stone, wood or brick houses with steeply pitched gambrel roofs (a roof with two slopes, the lower one steeper and sometimes flared). These sometimes reached down beyond the building to provide shelter for the porch. Flared eaves, seen especially in southern New York and in New Jersey, protected the walls from rain.

Town houses were usually four or five stories tall, with the owner living above his ground floor shop. The front door was often divided into two parts, to admit air and light but not roaming animals. Surviving examples of Dutch Colonial can be found in New Jersey's Bergen County, in Rockland County and up the Hudson River in New York State, and in Brooklyn, Queens and Staten Island in New York City. (MWK)

Dyckman House, New York, New York, 1783

LOOK FOR:

steeply pitched
roof with end
chimneys (above)

double-hung
windows
with shutters
(above)

gambrel roof
with short upper slopes

divided
"Dutch"
door

flared eaves
and roof
dormers

The Wren Building, begun in 1695 at the College of William and Mary in Williamsburg, Virginia, was the first Georgian building in America. The Georgian style, developed in England by Inigo Jones, Chrisopher Wren, and James Gibbs, was based on the Italian Renaissance vision of order, balance and dignity (as seen particularly in the works of the Italian architect Palladio), which derived from Roman models. As the American colonies became more established and prosperous, the leading planters, merchants, and farmers used English architectural building manuals and pattern books to construct stately and elegant Georgian houses.

Materials readily at hand were used in each region. In the Northeast, Georgian houses were usually built of narrow clapboard, often painted blue-green, salmon, or yellow. In rural Pennsylvania and in the Hudson River Valley, Georgian houses were of fieldstone; in the mid-Atlantic and Southern colonies, brick was normally used. In the North, central chimneys warmed the house, but in the South, end chimneys heated the many rooms in the winter and allowed the cooking heat to escape in the sultry summers. The Federal or Adam house, described on page 16, has many similar features, but it is lighter in appearance and less formal.

The Georgian plantation house, opposite, was built by the cultivated Virginia planter, William Byrd II, between 1730 and 1734. One of the most beautiful and gracious Georgian houses built in colonial America, it still stands on the James River in Tidewater Virginia. The view shown is from the river, as the house was approached in colonial days.

Hundreds of original Georgian houses remain in coastal towns and villages along the Eastern seaboard, and some particularly fine examples survive in Newport, Philadelphia, and Annapolis. The style's appeal is apparently enduring; builders continue to advertise fresh copies in many American communities. (MWK)

LOOK FOR:

symmetrical formal boxlike facade with hipped roof (above, right)

elaborate entrance

Palladian 2-story portico with pediment (found particularly in the South)

Westover, Charles City County, Virginia, 1700-1734
Builder: William Byrd

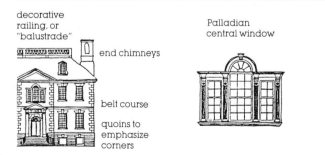

decorative
railing, or
"balustrade"

end chimneys

belt course

quoins to
emphasize
corners

Palladian
central window

keystone
lintels

sash windows
with heavy
dividers, or
"muntins"

The gracefully proportioned Federal or Adam style was based on the work of the Scottish architect Robert Adam, prominent in England in the 1760s and 1770s. Robert Adam had traveled in Italy to see Roman ruins, and he was inspired by the variety of room shapes and colorful interiors he found in Herculaneum and Pompeii. Roman decorative motifs of urns, garlands and sheaves of wheat embellished his reserved exteriors and classical fireplaces.

The Works of Robert and James Adam, published in England in 1773, gained the Adam brothers English clients and American admirers. American builders also learned about the Adam style from English and American pattern books. The dining room ceiling in Mount Vernon, completed in 1778, was the first American example of the Adam style. Wealthy American merchants and aristocrats in Eastern port cities soon built houses influenced by Adam. Elliptical fan lights over the front door, slender curved wrought-iron stair railings, and Palladian or Venetian windows provided delicate decorative contrasts to the elegant but simple rectangular or square exterior.

The Adam style has been called the Federal style because it was favored by the leaders of the new nation. Lighter in feeling and more refined than the earlier Georgian colonial houses, window panes were larger, but their dividers or glazing bars were more slender. Roofs were usually lower and often hidden behind balustrades. Rounded and oval shapes were more freely used. Typically, like Georgian houses, Federal houses were built of frame and clapboard with central chimneys in New England and of brick with end chimneys in the South. Many examples of these restrained and dignified houses remain in eastern seaboard cities. In the Georgetown section of Washington, DC, rows of Federal houses still stand. Some examples can also be found in Kentucky, in Ohio, and in other states settled early in the 19th century.

Principal architects were Samuel McIntire in Salem, Massachusetts; Charles Bulfinch in Boston; Alexander Parris in Maine; John McComb in New York City; Dr. William Thornton and Benjamin Latrobe in Washington, DC; William Jay in Savannah; and Gabriel Manigault in Charleston, South Carolina. (MWK)

LOOK FOR:

boxlike (or sometimes curved) shape, with low-pitched, side-gabled roof (above, right)

Palladian window on the second floor over the main entrance (above, right)

balustrade

stone lintels, often "keystone", over windows

belt course

arched windows in dormers

Harrison Gray Otis House, Boston, Massachusetts, 1796-1797
Architect: Charles Bulfinch

delicate ornaments
of garlands, urns,
or corn husks
(an American
adaptation)

slender sidelights
and elliptical fan-
shaped windows
over front door

graceful,
wrought-iron
handrails

Georgetown row house
with arched glass over door

The influence of Roman architecture in America came principally from Thomas Jefferson who used the Roman Revival style for his own residence, Monticello, and for buildings on the grounds of the University of Virginia in Charlottesville. Jefferson rejected "colonial" styles for their associations with England. During his term as Minister to France in 1788, he traveled in Italy as well as France, and became acquainted with the work of Renaissance architect, Andrea Palladio. Jefferson looked to Palladio for inspiration for his architectural work.

The Roman style, more impressive and monumental than the Greek style, was considered appropriate for major public buildings. The first U.S. Capitol, designed by William Thornton, typified the style with a projecting central pediment and classical portico, symmetrical facade, and shallow dome. State houses and court houses across the country followed the example. Roman Revival buildings are characterized by arch and dome construction, which differentiate them from the Greek. (DPF)

Monticello, Charlottesville, Virginia, 1772-1779
Architect: Thomas Jefferson

LOOK FOR:

round windows (above)

dome (above)

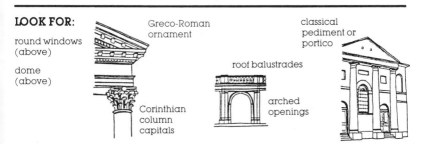

Greco-Roman ornament

Corinthian column capitals

classical pediment or portico

roof balustrades

arched openings

The "discovery" in 1804 by Lord Elgin of the Parthenon in Athens, the most important building of classical Greece, sparked a Greek Revival movement in England, which appeared in the United States twenty years later. The Greek ideals of democracy, beauty and simplicity were considered fitting for the new republic, expansive and proud, seeking a suitable expression in architecture. The country's founding fathers chose Greek Revival for many buildings in the nation's new capital at Washington. Early 19th-century architects Benjamin Latrobe and Robert Mills promulgated the style. Minard LeFebre published *Young Builders' General Instructor* in 1829 as a handbook for Greek Revival architecture.

Buildings are identified by a gabled portico or temple facade of one or two stories with columns of the Greek Doric or Ionic orders. Roof slopes are low and may be hidden behind parapets and heavy cornices; construction is post and beam. Perhaps the best known Greek Revival example is the ante-bellum Southern mansion. (DPF)

Cardwellton, Harrodsburg, Kentucky, c. 1830

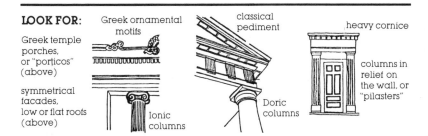

LOOK FOR:

Greek temple porches, or "porticos" (above)

symmetrical facades, low or flat roofs (above)

Greek ornamental motifs

Ionic columns

classical pediment

Doric columns

heavy cornice

columns in relief on the wall, or "pilasters"

The Gothic Revival style was introduced into the United States in the early 1800s. It was based on the picturesque medieval architecture of France, England and other western European countries from the 11th to the 14th centuries. Although used primarily for churches, it was popularized for residences by architect Andrew Jackson Downing with the publication of his book, *The Architecture of Country Houses*, in 1850. The style was an outgrowth of a romantic period of art and literature, typified by the novels of Sir Walter Scott.

Although rare in its pure form in America, the style was adapted in a variety of ways in the 19th and 20th centuries. With the invention of the jigsaw, Carpenter Gothic Flourished in ornate country houses, many copied from Downing's book. Ruskinian Gothic, influenced by the writings of John Ruskin in England, used polychromatic brick and stone in contrasting pattern and color. Victorian Gothic was a more eclectic style borrowing from Italian and German examples. At the turn of the century, Collegiate Gothic became the fashion for such college campuses as Princeton and Duke Universities. Many churches have been built in the Gothic style, foremost among which is the National Cathedral in Washington, DC.

The leading architect of the early Gothic Revival was Alexander Jackson Davis, whose works were publicized in Downing's book. His major domestic buildings still in existence are Lyndhurst in Tarrytown, New York, and Belmead in Powhatan County, Virginia. These are outstanding examples of this romantic style. For Davis and other Gothicists, the picturesque effect was a more desirable goal than the ordered symmetry of classical styles.

The most commonly seen examples in the United States are variations of the Gothic cottage illustrated here. Many towns throughout the country have one or more examples, typified by steep roofs, ornamented verandas, and a steep central gable often decorated in the Gothic

LOOK FOR:

steep central gable flanked by smaller gables or dormers (above, right)

ornamented veranda (above, right)

asymmetric form

battlements

turrets

pointed-arch windows

motif and often flanked by smaller gables or dormers. Whether located along country roads or on city lots, these buildings usually take advantage of topography and landscaping to enhance the picturesque effect of the architecture. (DPF)

Rotch House, New Bedford, Massachusetts, 1846
Architect: A.J. Davis

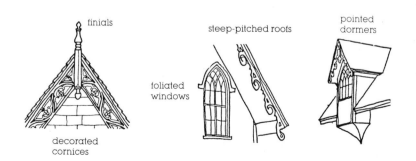

finials

steep-pitched roofs

pointed dormers

foliated windows

decorated cornices

The Italianate or Italian Villa style was inspired by relaxed, rambling Northern Italian farmhouses. Initially, it was adapted by English architects reacting against the disciplined order of classical architectural styles. It was described in American pattern books and, along with Gothic Revival, soon became one of the most common of the picturesque styles, which favored asymmetrical, towered, almost storybook villas in country settings. Italianate architecture with romantic allusions to a more pastoral past held great appeal in these early days of the Industrial Revolution. Andrew Jackson Downing, a prominent landscape architect and pattern book author, favored the Italian Villa style for "its broad roofs, ample verandas, and arcades" which he thought highly suitable for our warm summers. In his 1850 book, *Architecture of Country Houses*, Downing called the style "remarkable for expressing the elegant culture and variety of accomplishment of the retired citizen or man of the world." Its blend of classical and romantic elements also appealed to Downing.

Unlike the then typical white-painted American country houses that were considered by the romantics to be too glaring and unrelated to the landscape, Italianate villas or houses used colors of grass, rocks and woods.

Typical features of the two- or three-story house include square bays, a low roof with wide overhanging eaves supported by large, decorative brackets, a campanile-like entrance tower, and round-headed windows with hood, or "eyebrow", moldings. Numerous examples remain in the East, the South, the Midwest, and in San Francisco, where town houses with both flat front and projecting bay windows with decorative details are common. Many brownstones in New York City, and generous-windowed buildings with cast-iron, ornamented facades in that city as well as in Louisville, Kentucky, and Portland, Oregon, are Italianate in style, as are row houses and numerous small commercial buildings in cities and towns all over the country. (MWK)

LOOK FOR:

arcaded porches (above, right)

low gabled roof, with
very wide overhanging eaves
and decorative brackets
(above, right)

cast-iron
front

cupola

arched, tall windows
with hood moldings

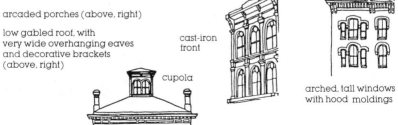

Bonneville House, Fort Smith, Arkansas, 1880

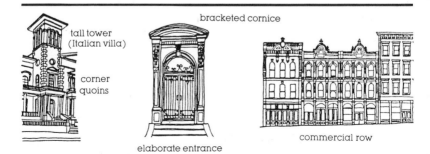

tall tower
(Italian villa)

corner
quoins

bracketed cornice

elaborate entrance

commercial row

24 **SECOND EMPIRE:** 1855-1885

The Second Empire — or Deuxieme Empire for those who prefer the French version — is often considered the "high style" of the Victorian era. It was inspired by Parisian architecture of the second half of the 19th century. The Emperor Napoleon III hired Austrian engineer Baron Georges Eugene Haussmann to carry out a program of clearance and redevelopment to make Paris the world's most fashionable city. Two subsequent expositions in Paris in 1855 and 1867 attracted many visitors and popularized the new French style.

Baron Haussmann invited Alfred Mullett, architect of the U.S. Treasury building, to bring a group of prominent American architects to the Paris Exposition of 1867 as guests of the French government. Mullett returned to design, in the new style, the State, War, and Navy Building, now the Executive Office Building, next to the White House on Washington's Pennsylvania Avenue. The building served as a proto-type for public buildings throughout the country for the next two decades, many designed by architects who had accompanied Mullett on his Parisian trip. The defeat of France in the 1870 Franco-Prussian war and the decline of Paris as the center of fashion caused the style to lose favor in the 1880s.

During the height of its popularity it was adapted for public and commercial buildings, museums, colleges, hotels and residences. The style is easily identifiable by its tall, stately appearance, and use of the mansard roof. Buildings are usually symmetrical, with prominent cornices and brackets, classical decorations, arched or rounded windows, often in pairs, and square, oval or round dormer windows. Wall surfaces alternately project and recede, often with central or end pavilions which appear as small buildings attached to the larger building, or towers extending above the cornice line. The style often vied with, and even combined with, the Italianate style in spendid residences for well-to-do Victorian families in hundreds of American towns. (DPF)

LOOK FOR:

mansard roof
(above, right)

niches, sometimes
with statues
(above, right)

imposing
formality
(above, right)

arched
paired
windows

iron cresting

prominent
cornice

Renwick Gallery, originally the Corcoran Art Gallery,
Washington, DC 1859
Architect: James Renwick

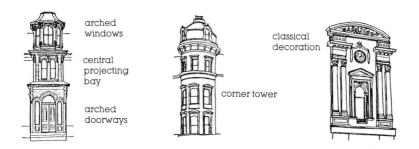

arched
windows

central
projecting
bay

arched
doorways

corner tower

classical
decoration

Somewhat Gothic in its tall, angular form, the Stick Style is characterized by applied horizontal, vertical and diagonal sticks to suggest the structural frame under the clapboard exterior. Expressing the structure of the building was meant to be a "truthful" way of building. Actually, however, the applied sticks only hint at the skeleton of the building and do not always follow the underlying frame.

Stick Style buildings were built with balloon frames, using light, closely spaced, riblike sticks for wall framing. Houses with balloon frames could be built more quickly with less skilled labor and at a lower cost than the heavy timber post and beam construction then commonly used. Balloon frames allowed more flexibility of form as 19th-century builders began to break away from box shapes.

The style is somewhat reminiscent of an Elizabethan half-timbered house, but its applied sticks are not necessary structural elements and can therefore be more delicate. Towers and long covered porches are common, and porch posts with diagonal braces and stick pattern railings reinforce the overall design. Steep intersecting gabled roofs and overhanging eaves are supported by large brackets. Its asymmetrical form, large scale, and use of color and pattern are shared with the somewhat later Queen Anne style, but its use of angular rather than round forms sets it apart. Not many examples have all the characteristics. In some, it is likely that as the original sticks deteriorated with exposure to the elements, they were not replaced. The Physick House, opposite, has been carefully restored and is open to the public. The Griswold House in Newport, Rhode Island, is a particularly fine example.

Prominent architects who worked in the Stick Style were Richard Morris Hunt in Newport (the first American architect to study at the Ecole des Beaux-Arts in Paris and, later, the architect of grand houses for the very wealthy); Richard Upjohn, who designed Stick-like Gothic

LOOK FOR:

steep roofs with intersecting gables and massive chimneys (above, right)

angular, asymmetrical shape (above, right)

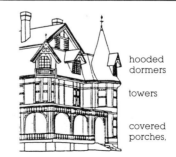

hooded dormers

towers

covered porches,

Revival churches in Maine and New York; the Englishman Gervase Wheeler, who lived and worked in Rochester, New York; and Philadelphia architect, Frank Furness. In the 1870s and 1880s, a Western Stick Style was used in San Francisco town houses, with stick decorations around windows and doors, and in panels above, to emphasize the structure. (MWK)

Emlen Physick House, Cape May, New Jersey, 1881
Architect: Frank Furness

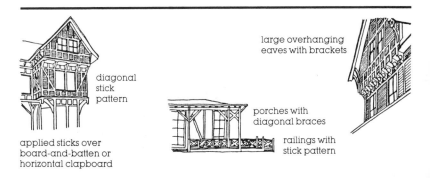

diagonal stick pattern

applied sticks over board-and-batten or horizontal clapboard

large overhanging eaves with brackets

porches with diagonal braces

railings with stick pattern

The late Victorian building style known as Queen Anne is recognizable by the opulent profusion of its elements — verandas and balconies, turrets and towers, varieties of materials, patterns and colors. The term originated in England to describe a transitional style of the 18th century characterized by attaching a variety of classical ornamentation to buildings of an earlier, medieval style. In America it satisfied the need of the newly rich of the 19th-century industrial era for symbols of wealth and success. It was the characteristic style of the "gilded age". The direct stylistic influence came to the United States from England most notably in the work of Victorian architect Richard Norman Shaw.

The style allowed for flights of fancy in the architectural and building arts, as well as a versatile use of materials and forms provided by power tools. Interiors were a departure from the predictable square rooms of earlier houses. Spaces opened and flowed, nooks and crannies appeared, and walls were paneled with dark woods.

The city row house was influenced by the Queen Anne style. The flat fronts of earlier houses were replaced by projecting rectangular or conical bays, grouped windows, and gabled or turreted roofs. These street-front variations allowed for more flexibility of interior design. The style was also adapted to small commercial buildings, often of decorative brick with terra cotta inserts or of multicolored stone. Many of these may still be seen in small and mid-sized towns. However, the most common use of the style was for large single-family residences erected by prosperous bankers, businessmen, and industrialists.

While wood Queen Anne houses as seen today are generally painted white, they may have originally been a mixture of three or four colors. From San Francisco to Cape May, New Jersey, many of the original color schemes are being restored. Overlooked in the first half of the 20th century by enthusiasm for other styles, Queen Anne buildings are once again being appreciated for their spirit of innovation and adaptable interiors. In spite of the name, borrowed from an earlier, vaguely related, English style, the Queen Anne building is truly American — an expression of the expansive qualities of the late 19th century. (DPF)

LOOK FOR:

projecting
bays
(above, right)

patterned siding

leaded and
stained glass

decorated
porches

Zimmerman-Wilson House, Annapolis, Maryland, 1891
Architect: George Barber

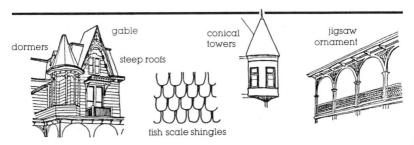

dormers

gable

steep roofs

conical towers

jigsaw ornament

fish scale shingles

The proliferation of building styles in the 19th Century led inevitably to combinations of elements of a number of styles in single buildings, producing a new Victorian Eclectic style. Inspiring this evolutionary style were the mid-century house pattern books which illustrated affordable versions of a "Venetian Summer Residence", "Gothic Cottage", "Persian Pavilion", "Tuscan Villa" and others. Builders or their clients often selected elements from various illustrations in pattern books, combining them all in one structure with a spirit of invention characteristic of the era. Their successes were dramatic, and even their failures are unique examples of the builder's art. Underlying the building surfaces, where a profusion of Classical, Gothic, Italianate, and French details might appear, was a solid craftsmanship and a mastery of materials and methods of construction.

The Philadelphia Centennial Exposition of 1876 brought exotic building styles, many with an Oriental flavor, to the attention of the public. Horticultural Hall at the exposition was a "Saracenic Style". Perhaps the best-known residence in the Victorian Eclectic style is the Carson Mansion in Eureka, California, built in the 1880s by a well-to-do lumberman. The house exhibits an awe-inspiring array of windows, gables, brackets, and columns.

Victorian eclecticism was expressive of an era in American history which valued inventiveness and individual achievement. Buildings of the period, looked on as gawky relics of the past for most of the 20th century, are now receiving deserved appreciation. Many, such as the Smithsonian Arts and Industries Building in Washington, DC which houses the 1876 Philadelphia Centennial collection, are being restored. (DPF)

LOOK FOR:

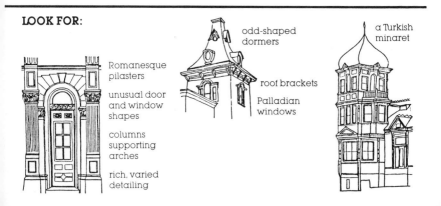

Romanesque pilasters

unusual door and window shapes

columns supporting arches

rich, varied detailing

odd-shaped dormers

roof brackets

Palladian windows

a Turkish minaret

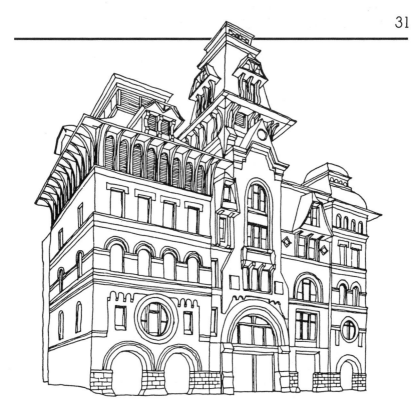

American Brewery, Baltimore, Maryland, 1887

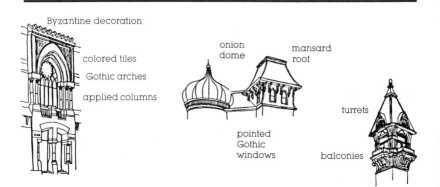

Byzantine decoration

colored tiles

Gothic arches

applied columns

onion dome

mansard roof

pointed Gothic windows

turrets

balconies

The Shingle Style began in New England with architect-designed, quietly ample, summer "cottages" for the prosperous. Rediscovering the simplicity of the shingled Colonial farmhouse, architects used the same natural materials in rounded, rambling adaptations for comfortable two- or three-story family residences. With its wide curved porches, steeply pitched intersecting gabled roofs, towers, and flowing form that follows the shapes of the rooms inside, it is somewhat like the Queen Anne style. Unlike Queen Anne, gambrel roofs with short upper slopes are often used, there is no applied decoration, and the house's complex parts are harmonized and simplified by being entirely wrapped with unpainted wood shingles. In contrast to the angular Stick Style, which emphasized structure with its applied sticks, the rounded shingle-covered house completely conceals its structural elements. Long sloping gabled roofs sometimes pitch down to the first floor, providing shelter for porches that encircle the house. Porch columns are often shingled, or of stone, and towers seem to grow out of the walls. Occasionally, the ground floor walls are fieldstone instead of shingles. Overall, the effect is of a relaxed, welcoming house, organized and assured, but unpretentious. Often shaped to take advantage of a view, its wide horizontal appearance, rough textured natural materials, and warm fall colors are at home in its setting of trees and stone.

New England seaside shingled houses by H. H. Richardson, McKim, Mead and White, and others were often featured in architectural magazines of the day, and some architects in other regions (including Lamb and Rich and Bruce Price in New York and New Jersey; John Wellborn Root and Frank Lloyd Wright in Chicago; and Willis Polk and Ernest Coxhead in San Francisco) built their own versions. (MWK)

LOOK FOR:

shingles covering an
irregularly shaped,
two- or three-story
house (above, right)

circular turrets and
porches (above, right)

leaded glass windows

angled gabled roof with long slope

roof eaves close to the wall

Isaac Bell Jr. House, Newport, Rhode Island, 1882
Architects: McKim, Mead and White
Partner-in-charge: Stanford White

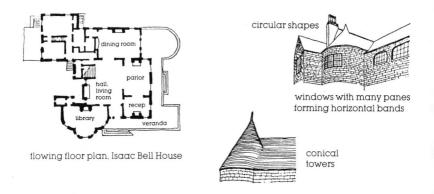

flowing floor plan, Isaac Bell House

circular shapes

windows with many panes
forming horizontal bands

conical
towers

Richardsonian Romanesque takes its name from the work of Henry Hobson Richardson (1838-1886), one of the greatest and most original of American architects. Born in Louisiana, Richardson graduated from Harvard University in 1859 and subsequently was the second American to attend the Ecole des Beaux-Arts in Paris. He returned to America in 1865, at first practicing architecture in New York City. After winning a competition to design Trinity Church on Boston's Copley Square, he moved to Boston in 1872. His architecture is somewhat influenced by the reserved and basic forms of early colonial architecture, but it is more reminiscent of the simple 11th-century Romanesque arched shapes that he had seen in the central and the south of France.

Richardson's robust masonry buildings announce power and energy, contrasting sharply with the restrained, orderly, classical revival buildings still fashionable in the latter part of the 19th century. His rounded arched entrances, towers, and uses of massive stone recalled distant times and places, giving strength and purpose in unsettled times. Commissions for new kinds of buildings, such as suburban railroad stations, public libraries and courthouses, allowed him to try new forms suitable to these functions. Those few houses he designed, such as the Glessner house in Chicago's South Side, seemed fortress-like in their inward orientation and severe exteriors closed to the noise and dirt of the street. Without applied ornament, his sculptural shapes are decorative in themselves with their contrasting patterns of granite and sandstone. Richardson was one of the first American architects to collaborate with sculptors and painters, and many of his buildings are enhanced by the landscaping of Frederick Law Olmsted, designer of New York City's Central Park.

In Richardson's time, a critic noted that Richardson's buildings made people feel secure and respectable. It is no wonder that his forms

LOOK FOR:

simple, low form with curved walls and asymmetrical facade (above, right)

short chimney to emphasize compact strength (above, right)

carving in columns

patterns of rough-textured stone or brick, with wall and entrance of contrasting stone were used all over the country by architects who wished to give a sense of importance to their clients. Some of these architects were: McKim, Mead, and White, and Bruce Price (New York); W. Halsey Wood (New Jersey); Shepley, Rutan, and Coolidge (Boston); Burnham and Root and Louis M. Sullivan (Chicago). "Riley Row" shown below is by Wilcox and Johnston, St. Paul, Minnesota (1887). (MWK)

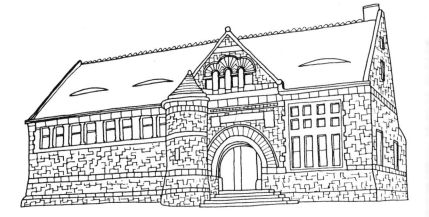

Crane Memorial Library, Quincy, Massachusetts, 1883
Architect: Henry Hobson Richardson

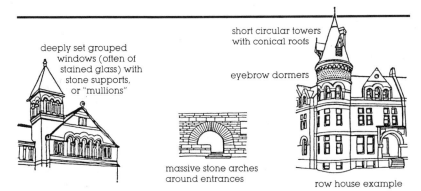

deeply set grouped windows (often of stained glass) with stone supports, or "mullions"

short circular towers with conical roofs

eyebrow dormers

massive stone arches around entrances

row house example

Although relatively tall commercial buildings of masonry construction appeared in New York and Philadelphia in the late 1860s and early 1870s, the first steel-framed, unadorned skyscrapers were built in Chicago in the 1880s. The time and place were right. Chicago's great fire of 1871 had devastated the city, and one-third of the downtown buildings had burned to the ground. To participate in the rebuilding, talented and ambitious Eastern architects were attracted to this Midwest city where offices, hotels, apartments and stores were in great demand. As land values rose, the elevator, steel-frame construction with terra cotta fireproofing, improvements in foundation technology, and wind bracing opened up new possibilities for design.

By the late 1870s and early 1880s, four major architectural firms — William Le Baron Jenney (later Jenney and Mundie); Burnham and Root; Holabird and Roche; and Adler and Sullivan — were designing steel-framed tall buildings, with walls of windows to bring light and air into every space. Bay windows and "Chicago" windows — a large, fixed central pane, flanked by two slender opening windows — were often used. Perhaps the most imaginative and influential Chicago architect in this period was Louis Sullivan. Sullivan believed that a tall office building should be lofty, "every inch a proud and soaring thing". Like a classical column, his tall commercial buildings had a distinct base, shaft, and capital. Sullivan embellished his simple forms with decorative entrances, spandrels (horizontal panels) and cornices, using geometric and natural shapes, never repeating his designs. Form should follow function, according to Sullivan. But for him, the function of fine architecture was to make life more significant, shopping more festive, factory work more pleasurable and healthy, and banking more neighborly. He is considered by many to have been a prophet of modern architecture. Examples of the Chicago Commercial style can be found in downtowns all over the country. And the simple, structural elegance of the best Chicago Commercial buildings foreshadowed the airiness and precision of the later International Style (see page 52). (MWK)

LOOK FOR:

flat roof with
deep projecting
eaves (above, right)

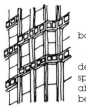

bay windows

decorative
spandrels,
above and
below windows

Sullivanesque
ornament

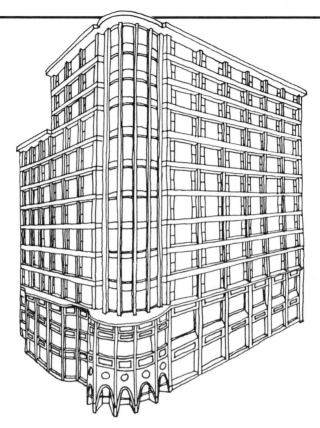

Carson Pirie Scott Department Store
(formerly Schlesinger and Mayer Store), Chicago, Illinois, 1899
Architect: Louis Henri Sullivan

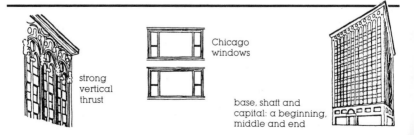

strong
vertical
thrust

Chicago
windows

base, shaft and
capital: a beginning,
middle and end

The Beaux Arts style was established by young Americans who went abroad, during the late 19th and early 20th centuries, to study at the leading French school of architecture, the Ecole des Beaux-Arts. In reaction to the romantic, picturesque, Second Empire style, the focus returned to classicism — Greek and Roman, Renaissance, and Baroque. The new architects returned home to devise a new eclectic style, combining decorative and spatial features of the classical styles.

Exuberantly displayed in Chicago at the Columbian Exposition of 1893, the style became the symbol of the City Beautiful movement, which swept the country in the early 1900s. Master plans for civic design by architect Daniel Burnham and the architectural firm of McKim, Mead & White, placed Washington, Chicago, and San Francisco in the forefront of the movement. Public buildings as well as private residences brought to these cities a new sense of formality and grandeur. The era of the Beaux Arts style has been described as one of palatial urbanism and included grand designs for parks and plazas, avenues, and boulevards. The term "boulevard" is a Beaux Arts contribution to the American vocabulary, taken from the broad avenues of late 19th-century Paris.

The style lent itself admirably to residences of American millionaires in the early years of the 20th century. Richard Morris Hunt, the first American to graduate from the Ecole des Beaux-Arts, became the favorite architect of America's rich and powerful. The Breakers, built for Cornelius Vanderbilt II, and Marble House, built for William K. Vanderbilt, both in Newport, Rhode Island, are examples of his work. The great substantial Beaux Arts residences, so soon to be unaffordable even by the very rich, survive today as embassies, schools, museums, or non-profit organizations, and recall a way of life now vanished.

Early 20th-century public buildings in the Beaux Arts style include train stations, libraries, banks and post offices. These buildings are

LOOK FOR:

flat, balustraded
roof (above, right)

rusticated,
raised first story
(above, right)

classical details

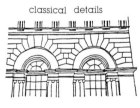

arched windows

statuary

characterized by dynamic shifts in scale and form, domed central portions, facades that project and recede, and application of classical ornament. The buildings are often arranged in complexes whose formal symmetry includes walks, gardens, fountains, and sculpture. (DPF)

Everett House (Turkish Embassy), Washington, DC, 1910
Architect: George Oakley Totten

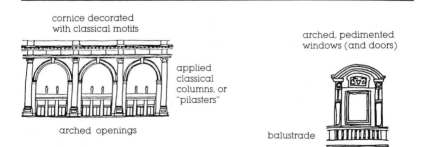

cornice decorated with classical motifs

applied classical columns, or "pilasters"

arched openings

arched, pedimented windows (and doors)

balustrade

The Arts and Crafts movement in architecture was primarily inspired by the utopian ideals of two Englishmen — John Ruskin and William Morris. Both believed that handcrafted objects of natural materials would humanize life, countering the impersonality of the machine-made. Morris urged simplicity in living, and his dictum "Possess nothing you do not know to be useful or believe to be beautiful" shaped a new taste for a simpler, more natural and democratic life. *The Craftsman Magazine*, published in the United States, spread the philosphy of Morris and Ruskin, and craftsman clubs in Chicago attracted the attention of Frank Lloyd Wright and others at the turn of the century. Charles Sumner Greene and Henry Mather Greene, who had established an architectural practice in Pasadena, California in 1893, became the leaders of the style. These brothers, who had studied manual training in St. Louis before studying architecture at M.I.T., were intensely interested in cabinetmaking, and they translated this interest into architecture. Using natural wood, stone and burned bricks, they built custom-crafted houses with large fireplaces, built-in bookshelves and cabinets, and handcrafted furniture. Sheltering low-pitched roofs, welcoming entrances, and comfortable verandas and balconies contributed to a feeling of a snug and intimate dwelling.

In addition to Morris and Ruskin, the Greene brothers were influenced by elegantly joined Japanese wooden structures and, to some extent, by Swiss chalets. Although Arts and Crafts buildings are sometimes called Western Stick, they are more horizontal than vertical, and the structural components themselves are visible, rather than suggested by applied sticks on the facade, as in Stick Style.

Architect Bernard Maybeck designed his versions of the Arts and Crafts style in the San Francisco Bay Area. The early works of Frank Lloyd Wright and the architectural firm of Purcell and Elmslie in the

LOOK FOR:

low-pitched
gable roof
with large projecting
eaves (above, right)

emphasis on
elaborate crafted joints

shingle-
covered
sides

use of stone

rustic
entrance

Midwest also showed craftsman influences. Although the handmade style was too costly for many to afford, it often served as a model for more modest houses. (MWK)

David B. Gamble House, Pasadena, California, 1907-1908
Architects: Greene and Greene

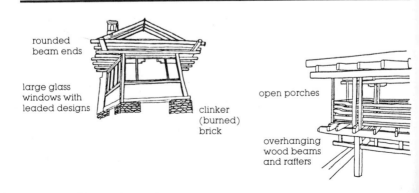

rounded
beam ends

large glass
windows with
leaded designs

clinker
(burned)
brick

open porches

overhanging
wood beams
and rafters

At the beginning of the twentieth century, Frank Lloyd Wright — perhaps the most original and influential architect America has produced — introduced a distinct new architecture, expressing the flat, sweeping prairie of his native Midwest. Wright loved the low, horizontal feel of the prairie, calling it "a great simplicity" that made the trees, the flowers and the sky thrilling by contrast. In Wright's words, "The vertical thrust gives a sense of power, but the horizontal brings us serenity and peace."

Wright believed in an organic architecture that united form and function and reflected the interdependence of man and nature: "A building should appear to grow easily from its site and be shaped to harmonize with its surroundings." Wright urged an architecture of simplicity and integrity that combined comfort, utility and beauty but did not imitate past styles. Ornament was not to be used unless integrated into the basic design. Symmetry was not a consideration, as the form was expected to grow and change as the life within changed. The architecture of the Prairie house met these objectives, especially in Wright's designs which defined space in dramatic new ways.

Prairie houses have broad, gently sloping, sheltering roofs with prominent low chimneys. Balconies and terraces extend in several directions beyond the basic house, creating protected outdoor spaces and rhythms of vertical and horizontal planes. Casement windows sometimes wrap around corners, breaking the barrier between inside and outside. Emphasis is on natural materials — the texture and beauty of wood or stone, or thin Roman bricks that reinforce the horizontal feeling. Leaded windows are patterned with colored glass. Wood strips on stucco walls emphasize structural elements and tie together vertical and horizontal planes. Planter boxes with flowing greenery and flowers soften the geometric forms, and colors of earth and autumn leaves contribute to a sense of harmony.

LOOK FOR:

spreading, two-story house with broad sheltering roof planes and central chimney (above, right)

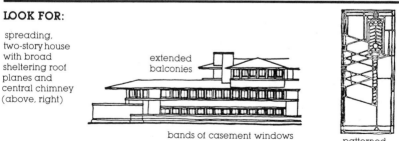

extended balconies

bands of casement windows

patterned leaded glass windows

Builders' low, ranch-style houses owe much to Wright's Prairie house. His architectural philosophy and achievements, first demonstrated in the Prairie house, have inspired countless modern architects in the United States and in the world. Wright himself continued to experiment with new forms until his death in 1959 at the age of 89. A major collection of Wright's houses, including his own house and studio, can be found in Oak Park, Illinois. (MWK)

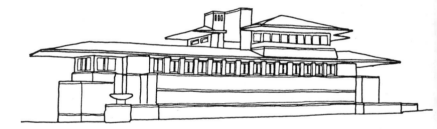

Robie House, Chicago, Illinois, 1908-1909
Architect: Frank Lloyd Wright

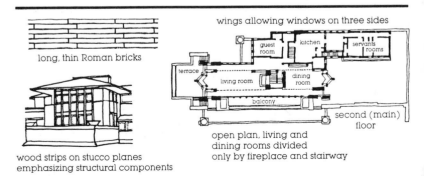

long, thin Roman bricks

wings allowing windows on three sides

guest room   kitchen   servants rooms

terrace

living room   dining room

balcony

second (main) floor

open plan, living and dining rooms divided only by fireplace and stairway

wood strips on stucco planes emphasizing structural components

44 **BUNGALOW:** 1895-1935

The Bungalow style was popular throughout the United States in the early 20th century as a dwelling for the middle class. Structures are usually one and a half stories high, with long sloping roofs, deep porches, and irregular room sizes. Although roofs may rise to as many as four floors, the image is of a low house using natural wood and stone to harmonize with the landscape. Characteristically, all living, eating, and sleeping functions occur on one floor, and may expand to upper floors, creating a variety of dormer and window shapes.

The term "bungalow" originated in India where low houses with verandas provided a central living space with surrounding rooms and porches for sleeping. These "banglas" took their name from the Indian province of Bengal, now Bangladesh. The British in Bengal combined the style with English cottage features, producing the bungalow form as it first appeared in this country on Cape Cod in the 1880s. Later it came under the influence of the Arts and Crafts movement.

Books illustrating the style and plans of bungalows were published widely, and multitudes of identical bungalows were built across the country. Many bungalows were ordered by mail from Sears and Roebuck catalogues and shipped pre-cut for assembly on their sites. Although regionally popular styles, such as Spanish or Japanese in California, and Colonial or "Swiss Chalet" in the Eastern states, were often applied to the basic structure, the form is universally recognizable. Typically, a veranda extends across the front of the house under a heavy eave line. A glass-paned front door opens into a sizable living room, the entrance hall having disappeared.

The style lost popularity in competition with the period revival styles of the 1920s to the 1950s, and had disappeared completely by World War II. These structures, generally regarded as architectural ugly ducklings in subsequent decades, are valued again today for their comfortable, practical designs, natural materials and colors, and harmony with the landscape. (DPF)

LOOK FOR:

asymmetrical
facade
(above, right)

combinations
of materials:
brick, stucco
wood, stick work
(above, right)

heavy
porch
supports

gable
dormers

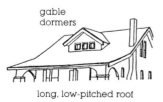

long, low-pitched roof

Bungalow, Hyattsville, Maryland, c. 1930

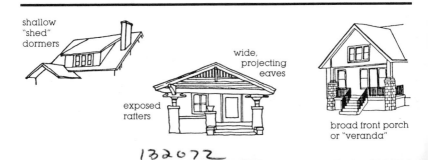

shallow "shed" dormers

exposed rafters

wide, projecting eaves

broad front porch or "veranda"

132072

The Tudor, or "Old English", style was in its heyday in the 1920s in suburban neighborhoods of New York, Chicago, Detroit, Pittsburgh, St. Louis and many other cities. The term "Tudor Revival" in American architecture generally covers the blend of a variety of elements of late English medieval styles, including Elizabethan and Jacobean. The style is identified by steep gables, half-timbering, and mixes of stone, stucco, and wood. These elements are often superimposed on otherwise symmetrical buildings in order to create a picturesque effect. The style disappeared in the 1930s but revived briefly in adaptive form in the late 1940s and 1970s. Large Tudor suburban houses, reminiscent of the English country house, blend with the landscape in form and materials in pleasant contrast with more formal, imposing, revival styles. (DPF)

Suburban house, Lake Forest, Illinois, c. 1925

LOOK FOR:

grouped casement windows (above)

tall shaped chimneys (above)

rough-finished brick or stone

steep roofs

projecting bays

Gothic details

half-timbered effect, either structural or applied

leaded diamond-paned windows

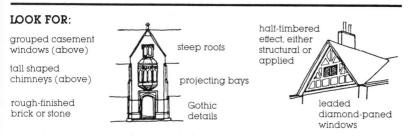

The fashion for adaptations of the American colonial house followed World War I and continues to the present time. Revival cycles vary between flexible interpretation of American colonial buildings and careful reproductions with different colonial styles as references at different periods. The colonial styles most often referred to are Georgian, Federal/Adam, and Dutch.

With its variations, Colonial Revival has been the dominant style for houses in the twentieth century. Forms and elements are mixed and adapted with greater or lesser success. Roofs are of a medium pitch and are side-gabled, hipped or gambrel. Windows are doublehung sashes with divided panes of glass, and often used in pairs. Doors are a dominant feature and may be flanked by sidelights and pilasters, and mounted by fanlights and by triangular or broken pediments. (DPF)

Hennessy House, Upper Monteclair, New Jersey, 1933
Architect: Arthur Ramhurst

LOOK FOR:

paned, shuttered windows (above)

symmetrical, flat facade (above)

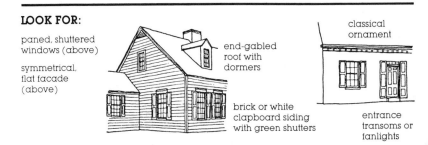

end-gabled roof with dormers

brick or white clapboard siding with green shutters

classical ornament

entrance transoms or fanlights

The French style in 20th-century America, like the Colonial and Spanish revivals, is an expression of many elements of French architecture of several centuries. The combination of elements is always unified by the dominant characteristic, a high-pitched hip roof. Based on precedents from Brittany and Normandy, the style is usually asymmetrical, sometimes with a Norman-inspired tower with a conical roof. Walls are brick or stone, sometimes stuccoed or with half-timbering. Popularly called "French provincial", the style is based on the country houses of the French landed gentry, rather than on the small farm or city dwelling or the great chateaux. Buildings are distinguished by a serene, formal air, through-the-eave dormers, quoins at corners or at openings, and low arched dormers. Another feature are "French doors", double-opening glass doors or windows which provide access to balconies, porches or terraces. The term "French provincial" is also applied to furniture and interior design of the same derivation. (DPF)

Suburban house, Dallas, Texas, c. 1960

LOOK FOR:

formal facade
(above)

symmetrical wings
(above)

high hipped roof

double-opening
French doors

low-arched
dormers

through-the-eave dormers

The Spanish Revival style of the early 20th century, also called "Mediterranean", was popularized by the Pan-American Exhibition in San Diego in 1915 and the work of transplanted Eastern architect, Bertram Grosvenor Goodhue. Adopted by Hollywood stars of the era, its architectural forms were popularized in films, and it was used for many building types, including western railroad stations, public buildings, movie theatres and countless stucco residences.

It is a colorful style, characterized by red tile roofs and occasional tile insets and facade decoration, by arched openings and arcades, decorative iron or carved wooden grillwork, projecting wooden balconies, and a sun-washed look of adobe or stucco exteriors. Plain facades facing the street are sometimes modified by intricately ornamental plaster decoration around doors or windows. Features of plans are the patio or courtyard, red tile roofs, balconies or galleries, loggias or pergolas, and asymmetrically arranged rooms of varying sizes. Although the style is associated with California, it can be found in most parts of the country. (DPF)

Suburban house, Phoenix, Arizona, c. 1940

LOOK FOR:

courtyard
(above)

balcony

red tile
roof

loggia

Art Deco, the fashionable style of the 1930s, influenced arts and crafts, sculpture and painting as well as architecture. It began with the 1925 Paris International Exposition of Decorative Arts, and was popularized in hundreds of movie sets through which Fred Astaire and Ginger Rogers danced. Its most notable architectural remnants are the Chrysler Building and Radio City Music Hall in New York, and the Old Miami Beach Art Deco Historic District in Florida.

The style is most easily identified by its architectural ornament, which includes stylized floral patterns and repetitive geometric forms incorporating sharp angles and segments of circles. Glass brick and rounded or angular corner windows were often used. Building entrances were embellished with decoration which extended to hardware and light fixtures. Glass brick panels were often lit from behind at night with colored lights.

The style found its expression in small apartment and office buildings in urban areas but has disappeared in many cities due to development pressures. Concentrations today are in New York, Miami and Los Angeles.

Art Deco has also been called Modernistic, Streamline, Art Moderne, Zigzag Modern and Thirties Style. The adaptability of the style to the skyscraper gave it a firm foothold in New York. From there, reinforced by Hollywood, it appeared in many places across the country. The style was influenced by Frank Lloyd Wright, particularly in the Midwest, and comparisons of Art Deco and Wrightian ornament can be made.

Art Deco affected product design, allowing for expression of new methods and materials in such products as the Budd Zephyr locomotive, the Chrysler Airflow sedan, and the Cunard ocean liner *Normandie*. New industrial materials such as aluminum, formica, glass brick, bakelite, and synthetic cork were used in design, often with theatrical, science-fiction effect.

LOOK FOR:

variety of colors and textures (above, right)

stucco and tile combined (above, right)

projecting sunshades

use of colored brick and tile

Rounded corner windows

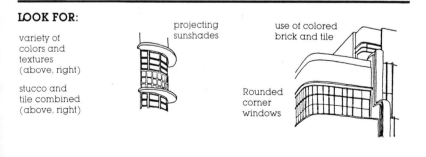

Art Deco fell from favor with the ascendance of the International Style, whose clean lines and white severity were a marked contrast. Buildings disappeared steadily, until interest was revived in the 1970s with the initiation of efforts to create an Art Deco district in Miami Beach and to save and restore the Chrysler Building in New York. (DPF)

Carlyle Hotel, Miami Beach, Florida, 1939
Architect: Kiehnel and Elliot

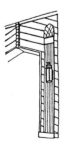

zigzag or chevron moldings and cornices sometimes reminiscent of Indian fabric patterns

molded metal panels or grills in stylized floral or geometric designs

The term "International Style", which has been loosely applied to modern architecture of steel and glass, derives from a book by Henry Russell Hitchcock and Philip Johnson, *International Style, Architecture since 1922*, published in 1932. The authors had organized an exhibit the same year at the Museum of Modern Art in New York, showing mostly European architects whose work contrasted sharply with the imitative eclecticism that they believed to be foolish and inappropriate for the modern age.

These European architects shared a strong interest in new developments in structural materials and an enthusiasm for the machine. Their fascination with simple geometric building forms coincided with the development of cubism in painting and sculpture. Typically, a steel or reinforced concrete structure of standardized parts supports a flat-roofed undecorated box covered with a skin of glass, or bands of glass, and smooth concrete or stucco. Often raised above the ground on slender columns, the white buildings of the International Style seem to float in space, independent of their surroundings. Glass meets glass at corners without frame or molding. Cantilevered balconies and white-walled interiors, with open floor plans and non-bearing wall partitions, reinforce the sense of flowing, unencumbered space.

These early modern architects believed that they had a responsibility to improve social conditions. With prefabricated, standardized parts, they hoped to make good housing economical and available to all. Richard Neutra, R. M. Schindler, Walter Gropius, Ludwig Mies van der Rohe, Marcel Breuer and other important European architects emigrated to the United States, and their ideas took root here.

LOOK FOR:

reinforced concrete, box-shaped building with bands of glass windows (right)

large expanses of glass, ordered elegance, floating quality (right)

Lovell Health House, Los Angeles, California, 1929
Architect: Richard Neutra

Mies van der Rohe's architecture in Chicago established a new mode for the International Style. Severely functional and carefully detailed, it is an architecture of contained minimalism, urbane and aloof. Glass walls hang like curtains from steel structures. Unlike the Chicago Commercial style (see page 36), there is no defined base, shaft, and capital, but a repeated pattern from ground floor to flat roof. In the late 1950s and 1960s, Louis Kahn developed a sculptural, expressive, functional style that has had great influence throughout the world. Many followers of the International Style have built monotonous and uninviting office blocks that eliminate human scale from city streets. But others, including Skidmore, Owings and Merrill, I. M. Pei, Wallace Harrison, Hugh Stubbins, Edward Larrabee Barnes, Richard Meier and Paul Rudolph have achieved some graceful designs that contribute to the energy and drama of city life. (MWK)

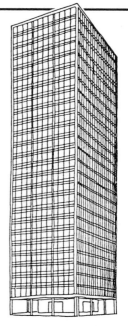

Lake Shore Drive Apartments,
Chicago, Illinois, 1951
Architect: Mies van der Rohe

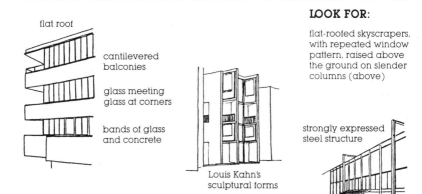

flat roof

cantilevered balconies

glass meeting glass at corners

bands of glass and concrete

Louis Kahn's sculptural forms

LOOK FOR:

flat-roofed skyscrapers, with repeated window pattern, raised above the ground on slender columns (above)

strongly expressed steel structure

In the middle of the 20th century, after World War II, a softer form of modern architecture began to appear, drawing its inspiration from the romantic naturalist traditions of Shingle, Arts and Crafts, and Frank Lloyd Wright's Prairie architecture, and strongly influenced by an appreciation of the proportions of Japanese temples. This form of architecture appealed to those who found the International Style too cold and rigid. It was called "Contemporary" by its practitioners, or "Bay Area Regional" on the West Coast, to distinguish it from the precise International Style.

The architectural forms of this style evolved from plans carefully tailored to clients' needs. Emphasizing natural materials of wood and stone, the Contemporary house was closely related to its site, oriented to sun and shade, softened with planting that reinforced its naturalness, and discreetly blended into the landscape. To invite unconventional solutions, hilly, dramatically beautiful sites were often used. Roofs were gently sloped and sheltering, with exposed beams and rafters. Sliding glass walls and wooden decks or patios on the back or side of the house extended the living areas outdoors but away from the street, assuring privacy. High, or "clerestory", windows and skylights were often used to create unexpected patterns of light and shadow and to bring the outdoors in without sacrificing solid walls where needed.

Early exponents of this casually graceful, comfortable architecture included William W. Wurster and Charles Warren Callister in the San Francisco Bay Area, and Pietro Belluschi and John Yeon in Portland, Oregon. Schools, college campus buildings, small commercial centers and clustered housing were built in this style as well as individual houses. Some contemporary residential enclaves were designed to include common land, and those who lived in them shared a sense of community and an appreciation for the landscape and for unpretentious designs. At its best, Contemporary architecture echoed the shapes of the landscape (see the Maine house below, stepping down the hillside, designed by architect Norman Klein), created strong rhythms of

LOOK FOR:

house nestled into landscape (above, right)

board-and-batten modules, creating decorative patterns (above, right)

sheltering roof

articulated post-and-beam construction

wood decks in the tree tops

post and beam, celebrated natural materials, and merged indoors and out with decks that extended into the treetops. Japanese modular proportions were particularly evident in the work of some architects. (MWK)

Johnson House, Los Angeles, California, 1951
Architect: Harwell Hamilton Harris

Japanese influences, modular rhythms

clerestory windows

skylights

balcony with overhanging sunscreen

house, "stepping down the hill"

Postmodernism began in the 1960s, as a reaction to the International Style of architecture, by reviving and mixing neo-classical and other elements. The style has been praised by some as contextual, as creating links with the past, and as an expression of site and tradition. It has been condemned by others as fakery — California architect Sym Van der Ryn dismisses the style as "the vacuous vagaries of neo-fashion". Architect Charles Jencks, inventor of the term Postmodern and one of its leading advocates, sees it as an appropriate expression of context, history and ornament. In a historical sense, a Postmodern building borrows forms from Greek and Roman architecture; in a contextual sense, it borrows materials and scale from buildings in its neighborhood; in an ornamental sense, it uses round or geometric openings, applied decoration, and even paintings of other buildings or scenes on flat walls to entice or deceive the eye.

The Municipal Building in Portland, Oregon, and the Humana Building in Louisville, Kentucky are examples of the style's adaptation to large, even monumental, buildings. More characteristic however is David Schwarz's Connecticut Avenue office building in Washington, DC, which makes good company with its neighbors and, except for its Postmodern facade details, might escape notice on the street.

The Postmodern label fits a great number of buildings going up in the 1980s. Separating those that are good from those that are not is difficult. The best ones will reflect, not copy, the best characteristics of neighboring buildings, and will make historic inferences by using neo-classic or other stylistic details in a spirited, creative manner. Color and form are important. In lesser examples, mere copying of nearby building details or historical architectural features can produce an undistinguished or unpleasant end result. The success of Postmodernism, like beauty, may be in the eye of the beholder. (DPF)

LOOK FOR:

asymmetrical windows (above, right)

whimsical use of historical elements (above, right)

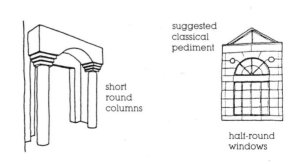

short round columns

suggested classical pediment

half-round windows

Trubek house, Nantucket, Massachusetts, 1970
Architect: Venturi and Rauch

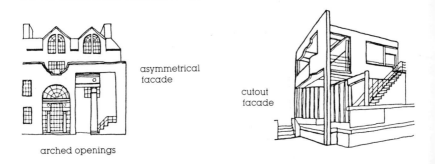

asymmetrical
facade

cutout
facade

arched openings

Andrews, Wayne. *Architecture in America: A Photographic History from the Colonial Period to the Present.* 1960. Rev. ed. New York: Atheneum Press, 1977.

Blumenson, John J. G. *Identifying American Architecture: A Pictorial Guide to Styles and Terms, 1600-1945.* Nashville: American Association for State and Local History, 1977. Rev. ed. New York: Norton, 1981.

Foley, Mary Mix. *The American House.* New York, Cambridge, Philadelphia, et al: Harper and Row, 1980.

McAlester, Virginia and Lee. *Field Guide to American Houses.* New York: Knopf, 1984.

Poppeliers, John C., Chambers, S. Allen, Jr., and Schwartz, Nancy B. *What Style Is It? A Guide to American Architecture.* Washington, DC: Preservation Press, 1983.

Rifkind, Carole. *A Field Guide to American Architecture.* New York: New American Library, 1980.

Smith, G.E. Kidder. *Architecture in America: A Pictorial History.* New York: American Heritage, 1976.

Whiffen, Marcus. *American Architecture since 1780: A Guide to the Styles.* Cambridge: MIT Press, 1969.

"In the United States it would seem that diversities of style and strong contrasts of architectural design are a perfectly natural occurrence."

Calvert Vaux
mid-19th century

To follow developments in American architecture and historic preservation, you may wish to join:

• The Forum for Architecture, an organization open to the general public and intended to stimulate public discussion about architecture. Quarterly magazine "Architecture", and newsletter.

> Address: The Forum for Architecture
> The AIA Foundation
> 1735 New York Avenue, NW
> Washington, DC 20006

• The National Trust for Historic Preservation, an organization dedicated to the preservation of sites, buildings and objects significant in American history and culture. Monthly magazine "Historic Preservation", and newsletter.

> Address: The National Trust for
> Historic Preservation
> 1785 Massachusetts Avenue, NW
> Washington, DC 20036

"When you look on one of your contemporary 'good copies' of historical remains, ask yourself the question: not in what style but in what civilization is this building? And the absurdity, vulgarity, anachronism and solecism of the modern structure will be revealed to you in a most startling fashion."

Louis H. Sullivan
early 20th century

"*No house should ever be on a hill or on anything. It should be of the hill. Hill and house should live together, each the happier for the other.*"

Frank Lloyd Wright
early 20th centry

"*Less is more.*"

Mies van der Rohe
mid-20th century

"*How can we expect our students to become bold and fearless in thought and action if we encase them in sentimenal shrines feigning a culture which has long since disappeared?*"

Walter Gropius
mid-20th century

"The house does not frame the view; it projects the beholder into it."

Harwell Hamilton Harris
mid-20th century